N0 BAD DAYS

a personal story, a method, and a movement... #nobaddays

David "DPB" Brooks

#nobaddays

Copyright

© Copyright 2019 David Paul Brooks All Rights Reserved Winfield, Alabama. No part of this publication may be reproduced, distributed, or transmitted in any form or by any means, including photocopying, recording, or other electronic or mechanical methods, without the prior written permission of the publisher, except in the case of brief quotations embodied in critical reviews and certain other noncommercial uses permitted by copyright law.

Scripture quotations marked NLT are taken from the Holy Bible, New Living Translation, copyright ©1996. Used by permission of Tyndale House Publishers, Inc., Wheaton, Illinois 60189. All rights reserved.

Scripture quotations marked NKJV taken from the New King James Version marked NJKV. Copyright © 1982 by Thomas Nelson, Inc. Used by permission. All rights reserved.

Printed in The United States of America.
ISBN: 9781672575577

DPB Publishing
www.worldofdpb.com

#nobaddays

TABLE OF CONTENTS

Acknowledgments	i
Foreword	vi
Introduction	x
Chapter 1 Understand the Unexpected	1
Chapter 2 Decide That Quitting Is Not an Option	9
Chapter 3 Master Your Responses	19
Chapter 4 Create Your Place of Change	38
Chapter 5 Know Everything Has Purpose	46
Chapter 6 Every Problem Has A Principle	55
Chapter 7 Keep Loving, Keep Leading	62
Chapter 8 Know Who to Trust	70
Chapter 9 Become Fearless	87
Chapter 10 Change Your Expectations	106
Chapter 11 "Blame Over"	118
Chapter 12 Master Your Thoughts, Master Your Mouth	130
Conclusion	l
About the Author	vi

ACKNOWLEDGMENTS

First of all, I want to thank God, the father, who has been my daddy throughout my entire life. I also thank Jesus, who has been my brother and taught me how to walk through this life. I also thank the Spirit of God, who has led me during this journey. Without you, there is no me. There would be no book, and there would be no ministry.

You are my ministry. You are who I want to please. In everything, I am striving to be more like you, and I want to continue to live a life that you are pleased with. Thank you for teaching me how to live my life with "No Bad Days," and I hope that this message that you placed in my heart and into this book will help others have no bad days too. Thank you for everything!

To my mom, Victory Brooks, you have set the example of how to trust Jesus, live for Jesus, walk with Jesus, rely on Jesus, and love people like Jesus. I am walking those things out in my life. Your legacy lives on. Rest in peace Mom.

To my sons, Dave Jr. and Fred Brooks, you have no idea of the impact you have made in my life to make me want to be a better man, a better father, and a better friend. This book would not be in existence if the two of you didn't love me the way that you do. Through all the struggles we have been through, I know that you are true men of God because you have never compromised your walk at one time through it all. You have heard me preach this "No Bad Days" sermon hundreds of times, and I am watching you both walk it out in your own lives. I am proud of you, and I love you.

To my brothers and sisters, my number one supporters, Stacey Scott, Carl Brooks Sr., Vicky Brooks, and Angel Hill, I am thankful for all of your support. I know my family has my back.

To my spiritual father, Pastor Raymond E. Allen Sr., you have set my course in learning the Word. Since my spiritual birth, you taught me that I am a champion of Jesus Christ. This book is based on your teachings and watching you. You taught me to go to Jesus for everything, and you taught me that the Bible answers all things. I know that so much in this book is a result of what you have taught me. I am a champion for Christ, and I thank you for being a part of molding me into that.

To all of my friends and ministry partners who have made monumental contributions into my life and ministry, I thank you. There are too many of you to name each person individually, but know that I love and appreciate each and every one of you! You have all made a tremendous impact on my life and helped me to make an impact on other people's lives.

FOREWORD

By Christopher Flaig

I first met Dave in 1996. At that time he was with the rap group D.O.C. We were at youth conference in Seattle, Washington. They were having a 3 on 3 basketball tournament and Dave was giving all his hype on the court, as I was, and we immediately engaged each other. I knew right away that there was something special about him. I knew that God's hand was on his life.

I was youth pastor at that time of group in the Portland, Oregon area. So, I asked him if they would be interested in coming to perform at our church. That was the beginning of, what I call, a kingdom friendship. It wasn't based on race or economical status or anything else, but the foundation of God's Word that says "love one another. As I have loved you..." (John 13:34).

It was from that moment forth that I was able to watch DPB up close and from afar. I was privileged to have a place at the table to watch a journey of one man's life, that went from mountain highs to valley lows. I have had so many open conversations with DPB of great success and daunting pain. Over the last 24 years I noticed one thing, and that was that every one of our conversation contained Jesus! No matter if it was about the doors the God was opening up or the valleys that Jesus was taking him through. Jesus was always the center of our talks.

I was so excited to hear that DPB was writing this book because I thought to myself, now the rest of the world gets the same opportunity I got to take this journey with him that I was able to over the last two decades.

No Bad Days is a personal story, a method, and a movement that takes each of us through a life that we can relate too. In today's world, where there is so much division and multiple information sources on the way to live, this book is solely based on the only truth that will stand the test of time;

that is God's Word. If you take the time to allow this book to rest on your spirit and mind it will totally change the way you approach life.

One would think it is impossible to live a life with No Bad Days. That would be true if you didn't know what DPB has come to understand, "with God all things are possible" and that we too can have this life.

INTRODUCTION

Never in a million years would I have thought that I would write a book entitled, "No Bad Days." I spent so many years feeling powerless and limited in my life in so many ways, but one moment changed my life forever. In the last eight years since then, I can honestly say that I haven't had a "bad day." Not only that, but I have taught the concept of having "No Bad Days" all over the country and knew that I needed to share it with the world by putting it into book form.

The funny thing is, immediately after I started working on this book, I was tested on everything I believed. I went through challenges in my relationships, my finances, and all kinds of things. I was even homeless for fifteen days! None of that shook me from what I have learned about living a life of no bad days, and now it's time for me to share it with you.

I want you to know right now, that no matter how defeated you may feel at times, there are principles you can learn that will teach you to come out on top every single time. You will learn that no matter what challenge you face in life, you never have to have another "bad day."

CHAPTER 1

Understand the Unexpected

One thing every human being on this planet has in common is that no matter who you are or where you're from, every single one of us will face challenges in life. Not only will we face challenges, but at one time or another, we will get "hit" with that one we never expected. Maybe you were a star athlete in school hoping to get a full scholarship to college but suffered an injury that was so severe that you can never play again.

You may be someone who has always done everything you could to be healthy and still received a cancer diagnosis. Maybe you always desired to have a house full of children, only to be told that you were incapable of having any. Some of you may have even experienced the unexpected death of a spouse or a child that you never thought you would live life without.

You had plans, you had dreams, and you had high expectations, but out of nowhere came that one thing that took you by surprise and shook you in a way you have never experienced before.

For me, that one thing was my divorce that resulted in the ending of my twenty-year marriage. Never in a million years would I have thought that I would go through a divorce. I grew up with four siblings and no father in my home. My dad left my mom to raise five children on her own. As I look back now, being a father of two sons, I can't imagine how difficult that had to have been for her to raise five children by herself.

I can remember overhearing her talking to my sisters when they were a little older about how all men were "dogs." After hearing that, I promised myself I wasn't going to be a dog to women, and I meant it. I was always careful about how I treated women even before I was married. Once I was married, I was fully committed to being the best husband and father I could be, and the thought of divorce was far from me.

Even while being in the midst of some of our most difficult moments in marriage, I never considered getting a divorce. However, there later came a time that it appeared to be my only option. When I said, "I do," I meant it. I loved my wife wholeheartedly and wanted the marriage to work. I expected that it would last forever. I was willing to fight for it, pray for it, work on it, and do whatever it took. I did all of those things to the best of my ability, but some things were beyond my control.

Many people, including our sons, thought that we were the ideal Christian couple. However, we were dealing with some very serious issues that they didn't see. It was frustrating to try to figure out the right thing to do. Ending the marriage would have significant consequences, but there was a point where staying did too. Eventually, the ongoing pain and effects of staying started to eclipse the consequences of leaving, and we finally decided to end the marriage.

The most painful part was the lingering sense of shock that this whole situation even had to happen. I couldn't understand why this was happening to me when I was so committed to being the best husband and father I could be. I wanted nothing more than to keep my family together.

I think we can all agree that no matter what kind of challenges you have faced in life, it's so much easier to deal with ones that you expect than the ones that you never thought would happen. When we know a challenge is coming, we can brace for it, and it softens the blow. When it comes unexpectedly, it has the power to knock us down faster and harder, to where the feelings of shock it brings can be the very thing that keeps us down. If we can come to a place where we understand that unexpected challenges come to everyone, and no matter how much shock and pain it brings, we are not alone.

Even though these kinds of challenges may make you feel like you're all alone, and you may feel like you have been "picked out to be picked on," you're not. Problems visit everyone at some point in life. Even if no one on your block or maybe no one in your family has experienced the same thing you have, rest assured you are not alone. There is someone, somewhere who has faced the very thing you are going through. Knowing this won't take all the pain of the experience away, it should help you in your journey towards recovery.

CHAPTER 2

Decide That Quitting Is Not an Option

Just like hot water brings impurities to the surface of the water when it gets to its highest temperatures, challenges have a way of letting us know where both our strengths and weaknesses are. Have you ever been so mad or so hurt that you found yourself saying or doing something you never thought you would? Have you ever been so low that you had to stop for a moment and ask yourself, "How in the world did I get here?"

It's crazy to think about how low I got after my divorce especially since I spent many years watching my mom be an incredible example. I watched her keep her faith through so many things, including her own divorce. Who would have ever thought that the same man who had spent years preaching and performing is the same man that was going home every night curling up in pain like a baby on the floor. Everything I had ever known and believed was challenged because of what I was going through.

The pain of the divorce left me feeling abandoned. All the back to back changes, the losses, and the loneliness I felt took me to a low where I had never been at before. I had to start life over in every way from the place I lived, to the car I drove, to the way I spent my time. It wasn't a change I wanted. I felt I had no control, and there was nothing I could do about it.

I was in that dark place for months. I had to learn to be alone for the first time in my life. Learning to live without my wife of twenty years, and my two sons was harder than I could have ever imagined.

    I was angry, and I was in a state of confusion. I was embarrassed and I felt like a failure. I had all kinds of things going through my mind. I was faithful in trying to keep the marriage together and I didn't feel responsible for the divorce. Yet, I still found ways to blame myself and kept trying to figure out what I could have done differently to keep things from getting as bad as they did. Even with that, I had to accept that it was too late.

    I also couldn't understand how I could be so successful at inspiring crowds of people to give their lives to

God and get themselves together while my family was falling apart. I felt like nothing I had accomplished in music and ministry mattered anymore. It all amounted to nothing when I looked at where I was at that moment.

The pain, embarrassment, and my distrust in people made me isolate myself. I didn't know who my friends were, and I didn't feel like I could trust anyone. Not wanting to get close with anyone and share what I was going through didn't keep me from trying to stay busy. I did this so I could avoid thinking about what I was going through, but that didn't work either. As soon as I was by myself again, all the thoughts were still there. I started to form what I call a "beat down" mentality. I was lower than I had ever been in my life. I felt like I was nothing and was even asking God what I was doing wrong to be going through so much.

At my lowest point, I got to a place where I entertained suicidal thoughts. I felt like my kids were doing good living with their mom. Despite what we went through, I knew she was a good mother to them and they had everything that they needed. I also knew that if I died, they would get insurance and never have to want for anything with all the money they would get.

I wasn't the first one in my family to contemplate suicide. Even my mom, the great woman of faith, was once at a place where she was so low after my father walked out on her, that she considered not only taking her own life but taking all of her kids lives, yes, including mine. She was pregnant and already had four other children, and we were all five and under. She was left alone and felt like she would have to do it all by herself, and at that moment, she was at her breaking point. She didn't feel she could handle it.

She was planning to turn on the gas stove and let it fill the house and take us all out while we slept, but as she reached to turn the knob, something phenomenal happened. God spoke to her and said: "Who are you gonna serve God or man?" That night she chose to trust God and live and allow all of us to live. She spent the rest of her life loving God, serving God, and teaching my siblings and I to do the same thing.

I was in the lowest place I had ever been in life and wondered if it was worth it to live, but that foundation of faith might have let me bend, but I didn't break. Through all the difficulty and the pain, I still remembered my mother's example. Underneath all my pain and thoughts of frustration and failure, I had lost all confidence in myself but always believed God was with me. I knew he was going to come through for me in everything I was going through, even if it didn't look like it at that time. No matter how tempting it was to give up, I chose to do what she did and put my trust in God.

When you get to a place in your life where you realize that you have let the pain take you to the point of no return, this moment doesn't have to be your breakdown. It can be your breakthrough like it was for my mom, and eventually was for me. The temptation to give up is going to visit us all. You may be tempted to give up on your marriage or your family when there is still hope. You may be tempted to give up on your lifelong career goals. You may be tempted to stop fighting that chronic illness or addiction that is trying to take you out. It may be that you feel the way my mom and I felt. You are tempted to give up on life itself. Whatever you face, you must press through and fight to win over that temptation by deciding that quitting is not an option.

CHAPTER 3

Master Your Responses

Everyone reacts differently when faced with challenges. Some people scream and yell, some cry, some shut down, and so on. Some people react for a few moments and then get themselves together. Some people have a tendency to drag things on for days, months, even years. In all of those scenarios, it is important to realize that the ultimate outcome that follows whatever challenge you face is, in part, based on what actually happened. What's even more important is how you choose to respond to it, not just at the moment it happens, but as time goes on after it.

It wasn't easy for me to figure out how to get out of that "stuck place" I was in as a result of all I had been going through. I had to push through each and every day despite the pain and the loneliness I was feeling. Eventually, people started showing up in my life to support me, and things started to get a little better. At one point, a friend of mine, who is a pastor, drove from a few hours away to take me out to lunch and surprise me with a bed. For the first time in months, I could finally stop sleeping on the floor. Not too long after that, some other friends came over and filled up my refrigerator with food.

Things were slowly getting better, but I still didn't have everything I needed to bring my sons home. At the beginning of December, I was praying for God to fill my house with furniture so I could bring them home for Christmas. One of my friends knew what I was praying for and decided to help. So, he took me shopping, and we bought everything I needed to fill my house up with furniture. Not only did he want to meet our needs, he wanted to make sure that we had things that we wanted, especially my sons.

He bought things he knew that they would like considering their favorite colors, posters of their favorite musical artists, and the list goes on. We worked hard day after day to get everything set up and in place, and we were able to be done the day before Christmas. I can remember the tears falling down my face when we were finally finished because I knew that all of this happened because God heard and answered my prayers.

I remember how excited I was to bring them home on Christmas Eve. I wanted to surprise them, so I brought them to the house blindfolded. When they were finally able to take off the blindfolds, they were in total shock to see our new home filled with everything we needed. That was a great moment none of us will ever forget. Both of my sons wanted to live with me after the divorce, but I couldn't take them right away because I had absolutely nothing they needed, not even beds for them to sleep in.

You can imagine how happy I was when I was finally able to provide a home for them. It was an unforgettable moment for us all, but the struggle wasn't over. We had everything we needed at that moment, but I was still trying to figure out how I was going to maintain it all in this new season of our lives.

When I was married, my wife paid all the bills and took care of everything. This allowed me to focus on my work. Being a musical artist and being in ministry brought in some income. Still, it wasn't enough to live off of. Especially not as a single parent with two sons. I had to figure out how or if I could make enough money to take care of all of us. For the first time in my life, I had to embrace the financial and practical responsibilities that were a part of taking care of my home and family.

Before I moved into that house, I didn't even know how to get the lights turned on. I was trying to figure everything out while also trying to figure out if my ministry was going to survive. All kinds of thoughts were going through my head. There were times I considered quitting what I was doing for all those years and settling down to become a youth pastor. This would have been great in many ways, but I knew that it really wasn't what I was called to do. Though many people would affirm me to keep doing what I had been doing, I just didn't know if it was possible, but it was my passion. I couldn't imagine having to give that all up too.

As time went on, I was able to continue doing music and ministry. I was so happy that I had my sons with me. We still had challenges, but we were together. That was what was most important, but I was still filled with worry. I wasn't sure if I had chosen the right home for us because, honestly, it was expensive. I chose it because I wanted the best for my sons, but I didn't know if I had made the best decision financially.

I also started feeling like my musical talents were being taken advantage of. There were people who invited me to come and minister and promised to pay me a certain amount of money and then broke their promise. What they didn't know was that I really needed that money to take care of my bills, and I felt like they just didn't care. This didn't only happen once. This happened several times.

As time went on, my heart was becoming harder. I became bitter towards just about everyone around me other than my sons. I would go do concerts and other outreaches as I had been doing for years and come home full of complaints, negativity, bitterness, and anger. I eventually got to a place where it seemed like all I did was complain and talk about people. I thought I was justified, and I had a right to vent.

In actuality, I was prideful. I didn't want to hear what anyone had to say. It didn't matter if you were a close friend, prophet, preacher, celebrity, or anything like that; It meant nothing to me. I felt like there was nothing anyone could tell me that I didn't already know. I was a Bible college graduate, and I had a spiritual father who taught me so much that I thought I knew it all. Keep in mind that I didn't trust anyone either. I didn't feel like anyone really cared. Even if I had thought they had something valuable to say, I still wouldn't have wanted to hear it.

I eventually realized that many people knew "DPB," the Christian Hip-Hop artist, but I didn't feel like anyone cared about or even knew "David." I wondered if anyone could see the deep hurt behind my smile, my performances, and my work in ministry? There is a saying that "hurting people hurt people." But, no matter how deep I was hurting, I was so distant from everyone there wasn't anyone I could hurt. I just kept hurting myself.

With all that said, God knew that it would take a very special person to get through to me. It would have to be someone that I deeply respected and believed genuinely cared about me. Little did I know, He was about to reach out to me through the person I least expected. That was my oldest son, Dave Jr. I will never forget the day he came to me and said: "We know you are hurting. We hear you complaining and talking bad about everybody. We know that this has been the worst year of your life, but you just need to praise God more."

I will never forget those words! I was stunned. I felt like I had gotten punched in my stomach, but it was a good thing because it woke me up. I was finally able to take my focus off of what happened to me and take a moment to consider my own ways. I realized it was time for me to apply what I had learned growing up and what I had been preaching for all those years.

The truth is that my son was only telling me what I had taught him and shared with audiences for years. The Bible teaches that God dwells in praise. (Psalm 22:3) I can't tell you how many times I would say to the crowd, "When things go wrong, you just need to praise God more because He inhabits the praise of His people. When we praise in the midst of whatever we are going through, He will come in the middle of our junk!" I had to admit to myself that while I was judging everyone else, I wasn't even practicing what I preached myself.

That day, I can remember looking up to God in response to what Dave Jr said: and I said: "God, I have had the worst year of my life, but I don't want to have one bad day in 2011." At that moment, I didn't have all the answers, but I had a change in perspective. I knew that if I wanted my situation to change, I had to change how I was seeing it and dealing with it.

I knew that I had to choose to move beyond what I felt and stand on what I knew. I knew that no matter how much "junk" I had in my life, if I would choose to stop reacting and start responding with faith and praise, I could trust God to get involved in everything I was going through. I knew when He did, He would start turning things around.

I grew up learning Bible stories, and no matter what I have been through, I have always been able to look back at what I learned and find something that I can apply to my life. I can remember learning about one of Jesus's disciples named Peter. He was known for being one of the most passionate and fearless disciples. Peter was close to Jesus, and at one point, looked at Him in his face and said: "I will not deny you."

I believe Peter meant it with all of his heart, but when Jesus got arrested and beaten, Peter was so scared he ended up denying his relationship with Jesus three times to protect himself. He probably looked at what was happening to Jesus and felt like he would be next.

Peter was a faithful follower of Christ, and I'm sure he never thought he would do anything like that. Still, the pressure of life and fear of his safety caused him to do something he probably didn't know he was capable of doing. If you fast forward a little bit to when after Jesus was resurrected, He had a conversation with Peter and ultimately restored him and commissioned to keep doing ministry.

Not too long after that, Peter ended preaching to thousands of people and going on to do amazing things. Peter was faced with a challenge that caused him to do something I am sure he later regretted. Still, he eventually bounced back and got back "in the game" and went on to do everything he was called to do.

On the other hand, there was another disciple named Judas. He also seemed to be a faithful follower of Christ but ended up betraying Jesus for money. Judas probably didn't realize that what he did was going to cause him to be responsible for Jesus being jailed, beaten, and crucified. After those things happened, Judas was so ashamed and distraught that he committed suicide by hanging himself in a field. Both Peter and Judas betrayed and abandoned Jesus. Peter chose to keep moving forward, and he ended up doing great things.

Judas placed "a period" in his life at the moment of his worst failure, but there could have been "a comma" with something greater to follow. If Jesus forgave and restored Peter, who's to say He wouldn't have forgiven and restored Judas. With that said, we know whatever mistakes we make in our journey are not beyond God's ability to turn them around and somehow work them for our good.

No matter where you are in life or what you are facing, I want to encourage you to choose to keep going. Make a decision to be the type of person that doesn't let what happened to you in a moment stop you from experiencing all the great things that are meant to happen in your lifetime.

CHAPTER 4

Create Your Place of Change

Things can either grow or die based on their environment. A fish can only live in water, and many birds can only fly in open air, and humans were created to live in the presence of God and never apart from it. When you think about that, it makes a lot of sense why there is so much death and chaos in the world. The world is full of dysfunction because humans weren't created to operate apart from being connected to and dependent on God.

Being dependent on God begins with understanding that He has all the power and the wisdom and instructions you need to live the life He intended for you to live. There is a scripture in the Bible that says, "it is in Him that we live and move and have our being." (Acts 17:28) There was also a King in the Bible named David, who said: "As the deer pants for the water, so I long for you." (Psalm 42:1)

If we want to get free from dysfunction in life, we have to get our environment right by inviting God in and depending on Him completely. This is why I had to be reminded to praise God more. By praising God more, I was inviting Him to come and get into "all my junk," as I mentioned in the last chapter. By praising God more, I was letting God know that I knew that He was bigger than what I was facing. Praise is an act of recognition of who God is and what He can do, and it is also an act of gratitude for those things.

    I know that it can be hard to praise God when it feels like everything is going wrong. From what you have read so far, you know that I have been there, but trust me when I say, complaining will only make it worse. Complaining will cause you to focus on the problem and not the one who can solve it, and whatever you focus on the longest will become the strongest. Praise does the complete opposite and causes you to focus on the one who can solve your problems. I'm telling you right now, it causes something supernatural to happen.

Take a moment to make a conscious decision to stop complaining and start praising God. You may not want to praise God for what is going on, but you can praise God through what is going on. The Bible tells us that King David said: "I will bless the Lord at all times, and His praise will continually be in my mouth." (Psalm 34:1). Bible scholars say that he probably said that at a challenging time when his whole life seemed to be turned upside down.

David was a "praiser," and if you study his life, he faced many battles, but he was also known for his many victories. I believe this was because he learned to praise God through everything, and because he did that, God always showed up for him. When you learn to do this, you will find that God will do the same for you.

It's also very important that you consider who you allow around you on a regular basis. If you are constantly surrounded by negative people who are always complaining, it will be easy for you to start complaining also. Have you ever been going about your day and feeling like everything is really going great in your life, but then you get around someone who is complaining about theirs? All of a sudden, you start thinking about things in your life in a negative light. The next thing you know, your both complaining.

It can happen that easy! That's why the Bible teaches us to guard our hearts. (Proverbs 4:23) Your eyes and ears are the open doors to your heart. So you have to be careful about who and what you are listening to and what you are watching. You have to be careful about what you watch on television because it can shift your whole mood and focus. Yes, it's good to know what is going on in the world to some degree, but you don't want to focus on it so much that it contaminates your environment that needs to be dominated by praise.

Even with that, it's all how you look at things. When you come across a bad report, you can choose to make that a time to begin to praise God. He is the one that has the power to protect you. He is the one that can direct you away from danger and into His perfect will. Psalm 91 talks about dwelling in God's "secret place," and all the benefits that come with it, and that secret place, is the presence of God.

CHAPTER 5

Know Everything Has A Purpose

At some point in life, you have probably found yourself asking, "why." "Why did I have to go through this or that? Why did I have to get into that car accident? Why did I have to lose my job or my loved one." The list just goes on. It's easy to ask yourself, or others, and even sometimes God, "why?" The struggles we face in life can very often feel like there is no purpose for them. One of the things that I have discovered while learning to live a life with "No Bad Days" is that whether it is God sent or not, it can be God used if you are trusting Him with your life.

I thought I had trusted God with my life a long time ago, but a few months after I told God I didn't want to have a bad day in the next year, I can remember him speaking to me. He said: "Dave, you haven't had a bad day, have you?" As I looked back over the past few months, I realized I hadn't had any bad news, and nothing had gone wrong.

So, I answered God and said: "No, I haven't." Then He said: "I'm going to teach you why you should never have a bad day for the rest of your life. He then spoke four words to me that I will never forget, they were: "I AM YOUR AUTHOR."

When I heard that, I kind of "got smart" in my head and said: "I know you're the author and finisher of my faith." Then God interrupted me by saying, "No, everything you have gone through since knowing me, I am the author of." He went on to say, "Stop trying to help me write your story. That is my story to write. When you gave me your heart and your life, you gave me your lifeline. Now, it's not your life. It's not your heart. But it's mine."

God was teaching me that life wasn't just happening to me, but God was behind the scenes "calling the shots" in my life even when it didn't look like it. That didn't mean that everything that seemed difficult in my life was planned or sent by God. It does mean that He was watching over me and strategically maneuvering in, around, and through me to accommodate His perfect plan for my life.

He helped me to see that He doesn't allow anything I go through to be wasted. He uses everything, and I shouldn't fight against what was happening to me. I needed to learn to "flow" with God on how He wanted me to deal with it.

When Jesus was preparing to be crucified, He made it very clear that no one could take His life, but that He was giving it, and no one could do anything to Him except the Father, "the Author," who allowed it. (John 10:18, John 19:11) There was even a time when God told me directly that there were things I was blaming others for, that He wanted to happen in my life just to teach me how to respond to them. I was getting mad! God had to correct me and let me know to stop blaming them because he was using what they were doing to sharpen me.

    Whether it is learning how to respond with patience and love when someone verbally attacks you or learning how to say no to an addiction that you have fought throughout your life. There is no area in life that God wants you to be defeated in. He wants you to learn and grow in your faith in Him. He wants you to learn how to handle these things so much that He will bring some of those challenges to you just to show you that when you put your faith in Him, you can conquer them.

Some people are deceived into thinking that having faith or a "prayer life" or even favor with God, means that you can pray your way out of ever having to face anything hard in life. That is not the case at all. Jesus Himself said: "Here on earth you will have many trials and sorrows. But take heart, because I have overcome the world." (John 16:33)

Regardless of why or how you suffer, God doesn't allow anything to be wasted. Each challenge you face is an opportunity for you to learn and grow and build your faith up to a place where there is nothing that can "take you out." The Bible also teaches that "when your faith is tested, your endurance has a chance to grow." (James 1:3)

The Bible also teaches us that, "God causes everything to work together for the good of those who love God and are called according to his purpose for them." (Romans 8:28) No matter what you face or how hard or unfair it seems, choose to put your trust in God. When you do, He will always work it all out in a way that you will come out on top! Trust Him as your author and allow Him to move the way He wants to. When you do that, you will find that your life will eventually illustrate a story of God's redemptive power and sovereignty through the worst of your sufferings.

CHAPTER 6

Every Problem Has A Principle

Knowing that God is your author helps you to understand that God is strategic in His guidance. However, knowing that does not make us exempt from responsibility in our journey of having "No Bad Days." Part of what God does is bring us to a place where we have to face certain things in our life. He allows pressure to be placed on us so that we will seek Him and His Word for the answers we need to conquer those problems.

As a matter of fact, what you don't know can hurt you. In the Old Testament of the Bible, the prophet Hosea prophesied to God's people that they were being destroyed by a lack of knowledge. (Hosea 4:6) The Bible also says, "His divine power has given to us all things that pertain to life and godliness, through the knowledge of Him who called us by glory and virtue" (2 Peter 1:3 NKJV) Finally Jesus Himself said, "If you abide in My Word, you are My disciples indeed.

And you shall know the truth, and the truth shall make you free."

Truth is directly related to freedom in everything we face. That is why the Bible tells us that we need to be transformed by renewing our minds because our natural inclinations are to our own human thoughts and will and not God's. (Romans 12:2)

The Bible also teaches that "a curse doesn't come without a cause." (Proverbs 26:2) There is a reason behind everything we experience. Many times, that reason is that we are believing, saying, or doing something that is opposite of the principle that God wants us to operate in to get the results we really want.

For example, you may be having financial problems, but you have faulty financial habits. Maybe you focus too much on making money, and God wants you to focus more on seeking Him. It may seem that you can't get ahead financially, no matter how hard you work! Matthew 6:33 teaches that we are to seek God first and trust Him to supply everything.

When you do the opposite, you may find that no matter how hard you work, you never seem to be able to pay for everything, regardless of how much money you make. On the other hand, when you seek God first, God will take your "little money" and make it go further than the "big money" because you applied God's principles.

You may have health problems. When you research the Bible, you will find that God addresses the emotional connection behind physical issues. For example, you can find that bitterness is connected to "drying up the bones," and hopelessness is connected to heart problems. (Proverbs 17:22, Proverbs 13:12) When you start consistently addressing the underlying bitterness or hopelessness, you will find that your health will begin to improve.

If you have a relationship problem, there is truth in the Bible that can help you overcome it. The Bible shares in an in-depth way on how husbands and wives should treat each other. It also shares how children should treat their parents. When you learn and apply the instructions the Bible gives in your relationships, you make room for God to come in and bring His supernatural power.

We must seek out that truth, learn the truth, and then be disciplined in applying that truth to get real results. You can also think about the truth you learn as seed. When you apply the truth of God's Word to your life, it is like a seed that will give you the harvest you really want. When you plant the "seeds" of words and actions that are not rooted in God's principles, you will have a bad harvest. With all that said, find the principle related to your problem. When you apply that principle, it will be like planting a new seed that will bring a better harvest.

CHAPTER 7

Keep Loving, Keep Leading

When facing challenges, it is easy to get into a "rut" where you are so focused on them that you don't consider how they are impacting those around you. It's important that you realize those who are around you are watching and even experiencing those challenges with you. If you don't take time to focus on and address the people surrounding you, you could unintentionally allow a "domino effect" to take place and not only knock you down but others too.

I was a single father during some of the hardest times of my life. I made a decision early on to do anything and everything I could to make sure my sons weren't unnecessarily damaged by the divorce. I gave them as much love, comfort, and guidance that I could. In doing that, I also had to learn to trust God, where I didn't have the ability or control. There were some things my sons were going to experience in life and face that were bigger than me.

For as long as my sons could remember, they thought that their mother and I were the prime example of a Christian couple. They never saw any trouble in our marriage. They saw marriages fall apart around our community and our church family, but never in a million years thought that would happen to us.

You can imagine how upset they were when I broke the news to them that their mother and I were getting a divorce. When they learned the "why" behind the story, it was even more difficult for them. It wasn't until a little later when I attempted to have a heart to heart conversation with our youngest son Fred, that I realized how devastating the divorce was for them.

Fred was angry when he first heard the news and did his best to avoid talking about it. If he heard others talking about divorce, he would walk away. I knew I eventually needed to have a father-son talk with him. I needed to give him a chance to vent and really share how he was feeling.

When an opportune time finally came, and we began to discuss it, he let out a cry that was from such a place of deep hurt. It was like no cry that I had ever heard before, not even at a funeral. It was so bad that day that I made a decision that I was going back to my ex-wife. I would have rather had to deal with the pain that came with our estranged marriage than to hear that kind of pain come out of my son.

    I really thought that was the right thing to do at that time. But it wasn't long before God corrected me. In many cases, reconciliation is an option even after the worst of breakups, but in mine, I had to trust God completely. He knew what was best for me. As controversial as it may sound, I know that He told me not to go back. He wanted me to focus on pouring love on my sons with everything I had and trust that he would step in and do the rest. I felt assured that

He would take care of us and get us all through it.

No matter what I was feeling or going through, I made a pledge to myself to keep my sons as a priority and become "Super Dad!" Whether it was making sure they got a hug every day, or had playtime with me, or just time to talk, they were a priority at all times. Looking back, I can see that the love I had for them and the love we had for each other played a significant role in us all getting through it.

Looking at my sons, who are now both in their twenties, you would never know that they had been through such trauma because they are faith-filled productive men making a way in the world for themselves and living out their own purpose. I realize that if I had pushed them aside and wallowed in my own pain, things could have turned out very differently.

No matter what you are going through in life, be sure to keep loving and leading others as a priority. If you're married, keep your spouse as a priority. If you are a parent, whether married or a single parent, keep your children as a priority and give them consistent love and attention and do what you can do, knowing that God can come in and do what you cannot do.

Don't let a crisis that came only for a moment destroy what are meant to be lifetime relationships. You may feel tired, depressed, and even incapable of meeting other people's needs at times, especially when you feel that yours are unmet, but if you depend on God for the strength to do it, He will never fail you.

CHAPTER 8

Know Who to Trust

I am grateful that I can look back at my mother's example of trusting God. Not only did she choose to trust God at the moment when she felt like ending her life, but she decided to trust God each and every day from that point on. My mom trusted God in such a way that my brothers and sisters and I felt like we weren't a normal family. I can remember her trusting and always believing that He was gonna show up for us no matter what we were facing.

If we needed food to eat, she trusted God. If my brother or one of my sisters were sick, and she needed to take one of them to the hospital, she trusted God to keep the rest of us. I remember a time when we were in a car accident. The damage to the car was so bad, you would have thought someone could have been killed! Yet, not one of us were hurt or had one single scratch. Her example was everything to me. She was always so thankful to God. I can still hear her crying night after night, thanking God for taking care of us.

I have learned how important it is to trust God completely. I know that He knows what is best for me, and His Word is failure-proof in guiding me. The Bible has many incredible examples of how important it is to trust God and how consequential it is when you choose not to. When people trusted God and His instructions in the Bible, they always prospered.

When they didn't trust God and didn't do the things the way he told them to, there were always consequences. I think that goes back to God being the author. When we try to write the story ourselves, it will never turn out how it was supposed to. When we let God write the story, things will always turn out better than we could imagine.

In trusting God, there may be moments when it doesn't look like He has written the script in your favor, but He has. There is an account in the Bible in which God instructed His people to leave Egypt, where they had been enslaved for years. So, they went, and not long after they began their journey towards freedom, they were stopped abruptly by the Red Sea.

To make matters worse, they looked back to see that the Egyptian army was headed towards them. They began to complain and fear for their lives, and some expressed that they didn't understand why God would bring them out just to let them die. They felt like God had left them, but in fact, God had set them up for total victory.

As the army got closer, God gave their leader Moses an instruction to strike the water with his staff, and as crazy as that might have sounded, Moses did it. When he did, God supernaturally parted the water. As they began to crossover, the Egyptians pursued them, but the water then closed in on each and every one of them.

As a result, God's people were able to make it safely to the other side. Then they looked back and saw the Egyptians had drowned. (Exodus 14) By trusting God, His people were able to experience an absolute miracle! On the other hand, we can also find examples in the Bible, where people experienced tragedy as a direct result of not trusting and obeying God.

In the book of Jonah, we find a prophet who was instructed by God to go to a very dangerous city called Nineveh. Nineveh was known for all kinds of things, and worshipping God was not one of them. Jonah did not want to go. He was so set on not going that he got on a ship heading in the opposite direction. God Himself sent a storm that was so bad it threatened to destroy the ship. People were questioning why this was happening.

Jonah eventually admitted that the storm was because of him and his choice to run away from God. You would think he would have just asked them to turn the ship around so he could go and do what God called him to do, but instead, he told them to throw him overboard. By natural reason, you would assume that he would have died as a result of that. Instead, the Bible teaches, God had prepared a big fish for him, and it swallowed him. He remained in its belly until he surrendered to God and agreed to do what He said.

When he did, he was spat up on the shore, and he went and fulfilled his assignment, and God turned the people's hearts in Nineveh to Himself through Jonah's preaching. If Jonah had just trusted God and went straight to Nineveh, he would have had the same result. Instead, he had to suffer things he was never supposed to experience.

When we choose not to trust God, we find ourselves going through storms we were never supposed to go through and stuck in situations, we were never supposed to be stuck in.

There can also be a temptation to put too much trust in ourselves to where we make moves in our life without consulting God. The Bible teaches us to "trust in the Lord with all your heart, and lean not on your own understanding, in all your ways acknowledge Him, And He shall direct your paths." (Proverbs 3:5-6 NKJV)

When you take a moment to acknowledge God before you make a decision or a plan, it opens the door for Him to come in and bring wisdom and guidance. This will ensure the best possible outcome in whatever you are doing.

I remember when I finished my album called "3-DPB." A lot of work had gone into it. It was time to release it, and God said: "Dave, do you trust me with your life?" Then God told me that I could sell CD's but not to release the album digitally. I'm thinking, "wow, don't release it digitally?"

Keep in mind we live in a "digital age" and truth be told, that is where artists make most of their money these days! Regardless of the thoughts and questions that came to my mind when God said that, I was determined to trust Him and do what He said. I knew that He had a reason, and that was enough for me.

So, I performed the songs and sold the CD's, but I didn't release the album digitally until five years later. God spoke to me to release it on my birthday, which was just a couple of months away. So, I did what God said, and even after already having performed the songs and selling the CD's for five years, I released the album digitally.

After that, God told me to promote my song entitled "Brighter Day." So, I invested a small amount of money into paying a radio promoter. Within a short period of time, it appeared at number fifteen on the Billboard charts! Anybody in the music industry would know that didn't make any sense.

Record companies typically invest thousands of dollars to get that much airplay and recognition. Because I chose to trust God, He did what no man could do. I did what He told me to do even though it might have seemed to be what many would have considered a bad idea.

Sometimes your greatest test of trust isn't with the struggles you face but with opportunities you face. God will test you with what you think can make you great to see if He will remain on the seat of trust in your life.

That was a test of trust and time. I not only had to choose to do what God instructed me to do. I had to make sure not to let the length of time cause me to change my mind about trusting Him. My spiritual father, Dr. Raymond E. Allen Sr. says, "When you learn to trust God outside the realm of time, you will get everything you need, all of the time."

You also need to guard yourself against putting too much trust in others. God can use people to encourage you, guide you, and even correct you at times. You should be open to that, but you can't become so dependent on it that you put them above God. This is especially important when you feel hurt by people or feel like they let you down. I have observed through life that people sometimes have a habit of looking at God like a person who failed them. Maybe you've had someone abandon you, abuse you, disrespect you, or just hurt you in a way that caused you to lose trust in them. But you have to recognize that even though people may have failed you, God is not those people. He has never failed you.

It can be challenging to understand this when the people that "did you wrong" are people that serve God along with you, but you still have to make a decision that you will not confuse them with God. No one should ever make you think that you have been separated from the love of God. (Romans 8:39) We have to remember that all humans are flawed without God. Even those who have a relationship with Him are still a work in progress. They have not had all the kinks worked out of their hearts and minds. So that you have to have fair expectations.

    Finally, make time with God because time builds trust. The more you spend time with Him, the more you will become familiar with His "voice," and the more you will trust His instructions. Think about it like this, the first day you meet someone, you're not likely to have trust in them at all. You probably wouldn't take their advice on things that are most important to you.

However, the more you spend time with someone and see that they operate with integrity in their life, the more likely you are to trust them. It's the same with God. When you spend time with God, you will learn to hear His voice and apply His instructions. As you do, you will see that you will always get the best results.

You will find yourself running to Him every time you need advice and guidance and celebrating victory after victory because He is trustworthy. He will give you wise counsel, and He never will never fail you.

CHAPTER 9

Become Fearless

God Himself has no equal or opposite. There is not anyone or anything that can ever be a real threat to Him. Many people consider the devil on the same level as God, but that is impossible. The devil only has the power that we give him, and his only real entry into our lives is through sin and fear. Fear comes to rob you of everything faith has the power to give you.

You must make a decision to confront it and conquer it! To begin with, you want to recognize that fear does not come from God! If it doesn't come from God, then you shouldn't receive it and let it dominate you! The Bible says, "God has not given us a spirit of fear and timidity, but of power, love, and self-discipline." (2 Timothy 1:7) In another translation, the same scripture ends with "power, love, and a sound mind."

Where does fear come from? The first time we read about fear in the Bible is immediately after sin showed up in the Garden of Eden. (Genesis 3:10) This shows us that fear is a direct result of sin. Sin takes you out of the position of loving, trusting, and depending on God. He wants you to trust in Him more than anyone!

He wants to be your first go-to when you need instructions, and He wants to be your most trusted advisor. With that said, let's take a look at Psalm 91, which teaches the importance of being in the right position with God. That position is "dwelling" in what the Bible calls "His shelter." Some translations call it His "secret place."

Let's have a look;

¹Those who live in the shelter of the Most High will find rest in the shadow of the Almighty. ²This I declare about the Lord: He alone is my refuge, my place of safety; he is my God, and I trust Him. ³For he will rescue you from every trap and protect you from deadly disease. ⁴He will cover you with His feathers. He will shelter you with His wings. His faithful promises are your armor and protection. ⁵Do not be afraid of the terrors of the night, nor the arrow that flies in the day. ⁶Do not dread the disease that stalks in darkness, nor the disaster that

strikes at midday. ⁷Though a thousand fall at your side, though ten thousand are dying around you, these evils will not touch you. ⁸Just open your eyes, and see how the wicked are punished. ⁹If you make the Lord your refuge, if you make the Most High your shelter, ¹⁰no evil will conquer you; no plague will come near your home. ¹¹For he will order His angels to protect you wherever you go. ¹²They will hold you up with their hands so you won't even hurt your foot on a stone. ¹³You will trample upon lions and cobras; you will crush fierce lions and serpents under your feet! ¹⁴The Lord says, 'I will rescue those who love me. I will protect those who trust in my name. ¹⁵ When they call on me, I will answer; I will be with them in trouble. I will rescue and honor them. ¹⁶I will reward them with a long life and give them my salvation. (Psalm 91)

When you're intentional about spending time in the presence of God, you're placing yourself in His "secret place." In other words, in His shelter. You can't get "into" this kind of place with God through religion and tradition.

You get into this kind of place with God based on your heart's position with Him. That must be a position of surrender, devotion, and total dependence on Him. This is not a one-time thing. You must bring yourself into that position and keep yourself there.

When problems show up in your life, the first thing you should do is ask yourself if you have been dwelling in the secret place. You should take inventory of your life and consider how much time and effort you have invested in your pursuit of God and His presence. If you find that someone or something has distracted you from that pursuit, you can just about guarantee that area of your life will be challenged by God at some point. This happens to draw you back into the place where you need to be, and that again is a place of total surrender and dependence on God.

With that said, many people have a tendency to run to everyone but God when they are going through something. Though there is nothing wrong with going to church or asking for others to pray for you, or calling your pastor, family members, or best friends to help you. They shouldn't be your first go-to, and they definitely shouldn't be your only go-to. No one can give you what God can give you in that secret place.

The statement "fear not" shows up throughout the Bible many times. This phrase is spoken through angels before communicating God's messages to man. Even the angels know that fear can block the ability for people to receive from God, so they deal with the fear before they deliver the message they were sent to share. (Isaiah 41:10, Luke 1:13, Luke 1:30)

Another example of God having to deal with fear before faith could operate fully was when Jesus was seen walking on water. He was headed to His disciples, who were in a boat in the midst of a storm. When they saw Him, they begin to panic. The first thing He said was, "do not fear." (Matthew 14:27) A few verses later, one of His disciples stepped out of the boat and began to walk on water too. After a few steps, that miraculous moment was disrupted because he began to fear and ended up sinking, but Jesus reached out and grabbed him. (Luke 14:31)

    After grabbing him, Jesus said: "You have so little faith. Why did you doubt Me?" I think it is worth pointing out that Jesus didn't say, "why did you doubt yourself" but instead, He said: "Why did you doubt Me?" That is a reminder to you that your faith cannot be in yourself or in your ability, but in God's alone.

I can remember in those first few years after my divorce when God was continually speaking to me about living a life with "No Bad Days." One day he said: "Dave, what if I told you that Job didn't have to go through what he went through?" I immediately thought, "What? Job is the first person everybody brings up when they go through suffering that they don't understand." You can imagine my shock when God told me his situation could have been avoided.

God prompted me to look at the Book of Job again, and this time I saw some things I never noticed before. God did call Job a righteous man, who He could find no fault in, but I was also able to see that Job was very fearful. (Job 1:8) He reverentially feared God, but, if you read through the entire book of Job, you will see that he also deeply feared loss. He feared loss so much that he would make sacrifices regularly.

Back in those days, people would make sacrifices as acts of worship and also as a way to ask God for mercy when they made mistakes in hopes that He would forgive them. Many of those sacrifices were made on behalf of his children because of how fearful he was that they might have done something wrong to provoke the wrath of God (Job 1:5). With that said, some of Job's "righteous actions" were motivated by his fearful heart. When trouble started to break out in Job's life, he said: "What I always feared has happened to me. What I dreaded has come true." (Job 3:25)

We can confirm that fear was definitely a problem in Job's life. This is remarkable considering that Job did so much to honor God, but didn't seem to trust Him enough to do his righteous acts from faith alone.

In Job Chapter 1, you can read of Satan approaching God and having a conversation with Him. He said he had been "roaming" through the earth, and then God said to him, "Have you noticed my servant Job? He is the finest man in all the earth. He is blameless - a man of complete integrity. He fears God and stays away from evil." (Job 1:8)

Satan, who the Bible also calls the accuser, responded by remarking how blessed Job was. He seemed to think that Job would change his position if God stopped being so good to him and his family. Satan challenged God to remove the "hedge of protection" (Job 1:9) from around Job to see if he would continue to serve Him after difficulty hit his life. What's so amazing is that

God not only pointed out Job to Satan, but He also consented to Satan testing Job within certain limitations.

I can remember when God said: "Dave, why do you think I would mention Job's name to Satan?" God began to speak to me about how fear could damage the hedge of protection that He has given His people. I have since learned that fear has the power to open your life up to all kinds of things that you were never meant to experience.

As you study the story of Job in-depth, though you will never find him cursing God as Satan had assumed he would, you will see that he struggled deeply with trust in God and the fear of loss. Job complained and challenged God so much that at one point, God responded to Job and said:

> [2] Who is this that questions my wisdom with such ignorant words? [3] Brace yourself like a man, because I have some questions for you, and you must answer them. [4] "Where were you when I laid the foundations of the earth? Tell me, if you know so much [5] who determined its dimensions and stretched out the surveying line? [6] What supports its foundations, and who laid its

cornerstone [7] as the morning stars sang together and all the angels[a] shouted for joy? (Job 38:1-7)

Scripture goes on and on detailing the powerful creative work and strategy of God in the earth in such a way that we may say put Job back in his place. God counter challenged Job's distrust by challenging him as to who he was to doubt His sovereignty. Though I can't say for sure, the pressure in Job's life brought all that distrust to the surface, but God knew it was always there. That may have been why God allowed Job to be challenged the way he was.

It's easy to talk about Job, but fear is something that tries everybody at some point in life. The good news is there is an answer. The Bible says, "perfect love expels all fear." (1 John 4:18) The key that is going to unlock you from the grip of fear is learning to be perfected in love. You need to spend time learning about and meditating on God's love for you. When you trust in His heart towards you, you will have faith concerning His plans and His actions towards you.

Eventually, fear will have no place. Think about it like this: when you believe someone truly loves you, you have no expectation for them to harm you or leave you. When you learn to believe in how much God loves you, then you will learn to feel the same way about Him.

CHAPTER 10

Change Your Expectations

It is easy to start expecting negative things to happen to you if you have experienced a lot of challenges throughout your life. While it is good to understand that challenges are a part of the human experience and not be completely shocked when they show up; It's a terrible thing to allow life to beat you down so bad that you begin to expect them to come all the time and never end! Have you ever found yourself saying things like, "it never stops," or "why can't I ever win or get ahead?" If you have, then you were suffering from negative expectations.

Years ago, I can remember that I would get my taxes done and have a return due to me. I would always say, "Why when I get my check, something bad always gotta happen." Without fail, every year after that, it did, and I never had money left over. Eventually, as I grew in my relationship with God, I realized that this was happening, because I expected it to happen! I changed my expectation to one of faith.

I chose to believe and expect that no challenges would show up at the same time that my tax return did. After I did that, it never happened again, and I was able to spend the money the way I wanted to.

I remember a time when a friend of mine who had been diagnosed with cancer and later recovered, formed a bump on his lip. As soon as the bump showed up before he had a chance to go to the doctor, he already assumed it was cancer. When he went to the doctor, he found out it wasn't cancer at all.

That little bump caused him to expect the worst possible scenario. Now, this will probably sound ridiculous, but there was a time in my life when I would sneeze and see "stars." I believed it was a sign that something terrible was about to happen, and because I expected it, it always would.

It can be easy to get caught in a cycle of negative expectations, but you don't have to be stuck in that cycle anymore. Next time you start rehearsing negative expectations in your mind, stop and ask yourself why you are thinking what you are thinking? Why are you expecting what you are expecting? Maybe you are someone who has watched family member after family member become sick and possibly even lose their life as a result of a disease. So, you assume that it will happen to you. I am here to tell you; it doesn't have to!

Maybe you are someone who is a part of a family that has suffered in poverty for generations and never been able to get free from debt. You don't have to expect that cycle to continue with you. If you're going to be a person of faith, why not have faith in God to show up and cause you to become that one that defies the odds every time.

Expectations are like magnets that pull stuff into and out of your life without you realizing it. You want to make sure that your expectations are bringing you the right things. Every story I have read in the Bible where someone expected God to show up for them, He did.

One of the most well-known examples of this kind of expectation can be found in the Bible in the book of Daniel. Three young boys had chosen to honor God above their very own lives by refusing to bow down to a golden image or serve another "god." Because of this, they were thrown into a furnace to be burned alive. Even when faced with death, they stayed true to their faith in God, but right before it happened, they declared that God was able to show up even in the threat of being burnt alive. Not only did they survive the fire that they were thrown into, but the heat from that fire caused the guards to die. Others who were watching said that they saw a fourth man in the fire who looked like "the son of God."

In 1 Samuel 1:17, you can read about a time when God's people were being threatened and tormented by a giant named Goliath. Goliath was so scary no one wanted to challenge him, not even their king, who was known as a warrior. One day a shepherd boy named David, who was known at that time for keeping his father's sheep, showed up on the scene ready to challenge that giant.

David had been fighting lions and bears during his time tending his father's sheep and developed so much confidence in God that he believed he could take the giant. Before he went to challenge Goliath, he asked what the reward was gonna be for the one who defeats him. I believe David was so sure that God was going to show up for him as he stood up to that giant that he went ahead and found out what he was gonna get for it!

He had full expectation that he would win, not because of his own strength, or his own ability, but because of his faith in God. He took Goliath out by striking him with one smooth stone and then took his own sword to cut off his head.

In the book of Matthew, Jesus demonstrated the power of expectation to us when he touched the blind eyes of a couple of men and told them that they would receive their healing according to their faith. Later on, in Matthew, the Bible tells us that there was a place he couldn't do many miracles because of their lack of faith. A lack of faith is ultimately a lack of expectation.

Another account in the Bible shares about a man who heard Jesus was in town and was going all over town crying out for Jesus. Finally, Jesus called for him, and when that happened, that man got up and cast aside his garment, which Bible scholars say identified him as blind. He then went after Jesus in expectation of getting his healing. He expected to be healed when he came into the presence of Jesus and was so confident that he knew he would no longer need that garment. (Mark 10)

It's easy to think that there are predetermined outcomes, and things are just going to be what they are going to be, and what we are going to experience in life that can't be changed, but based on what the Bible teaches, your expectation can change your entire situation.

It's time for you to put negative expectations to rest and start to believe and expect God to show up for you every time you face a challenge. If you look at everyday life, you sit down on a chair without checking its strength because you expect that it was created for you to sit safely in.

You turn on the ignition in the car and start driving because you trust that the car is going to do what it was created to do. You put expensive gifts in boxes and send them through the postal service because you expect that they are going to make it to their destination. In the same way, you should expect that when you put your faith in God and expect Him to show up, He will!

No matter how dark, lifeless, or hopeless what you face looks like. God can show up and work it for your good and cause you to get victory out of it.

CHAPTER 11

"Blame Over"

It can be easy to blame others when things don't go the way you wanted them to go. Maybe you weren't raised in the best neighborhood or you didn't have much support from your parents when you were growing up. You may have been in an accident that gave you injuries that caused a ripple effect of problems in your life. Maybe you went through a divorce that seemed to destroy your life as you knew it.

You may have even been abandoned, neglected, violated, or abused by someone. No matter what your story is, it's very likely that at some point in your journey, you have wanted to blame someone for why your life turned out the way it did.

There have been times when I have blamed others for things that seemed to have gone wrong in my life. Many people I thought would be in my life forever didn't stick around. There have been people I trusted who betrayed me. I have even blamed others for not opening doors for me that could have changed my life.

There are times I even doubted and blamed myself for some of those very things. I felt like there had to be something wrong with me for things to not go my way. Looking back now, I understand that no one can stand in the way of what God truly has for me, and nothing can touch my life without God's permission, so there is no reason for me to blame anyone or anything for what I have experienced or where I am in life.

Here is an example. Years ago, I had to move from Baltimore, Maryland, to Birmingham, Alabama. I was a part of a ministry team that served at a church in Baltimore, and there came a time we felt God leading us somewhere else.

We went to the pastor to let him know that we felt that it was our time to go and move into our next phase in life and ministry. However, the pastor was very direct with us. He told us if anybody left his church as a result of us leaving, he was going to curse our ministry "forever," and he said that we would never minister in another church again. He eventually demanded that we sign a contract that committed us to go to another church that he consented to. This was the only way he would "release us" from his leadership. I thought he was "buggin out!" I couldn't believe that he wanted us to sign a contract and move all the way to Birmingham, Alabama! I was beyond mad. I didn't feel God was in it at all. At first, I didn't want to go and didn't have any plans to go because I knew that we didn't do anything wrong.

I wasn't planning to sign anything, and I was definitely not going to let that pastor force me to leave the city that God led me to. Despite how I was feeling, I eventually gave in. I signed the contracts along with everyone else and we all, moved to Alabama just so we could move on with our lives.

When we got to Alabama, we submitted ourselves to that new church while still dealing with mixed feelings about the whole situation. We served there, and we did our best to honor God despite how we felt. I was constantly saying to myself, "I trust you God, but what am I doing here?"

Little did I know, I was about to walk through one of the biggest doors I had ever walked through and begin ministering to thousands of people in Alabama by becoming a part of one of the largest youth movements in America at that time. Looking back, I see it was all a setup. It looked like a terrible situation, but it actually positioned me for what God had for me next.

Another example is when I was a part of a music group that broke up. I was really disappointed at first. Now I realize that was a catalyst for me to find my personal identity as an artist and to become known as DPB, which I am still known by today. Later down the road, another shift in my life caused my two sons to start performing with me, and the list goes on.

I am sure you can understand why I wanted to blame people for the things that I went through, but after seeing God work everything out in my favor time after time, I knew I had to let it all go. I can remember when God told me to find everyone I could from my past that I had either offended or been offended by and tell them I was sorry.

Whether I was right or wrong, this was very hard to do, but I did it anyway, and I am glad I did. Looking back, I realize that doing that freed me from the hurt and the pain I was feeling, and the hold people had on my life. These are the same people I blamed for everything that went wrong in my life. To be honest, I didn't realize that I was depending on people more than I should have been. This was something God wanted me to deal with next.

As a result of finally letting go of all those offenses and choosing to no longer blame anyone for the outcome of my life, the focus now had to shift from them to me. It wasn't long before I realized that I also had a problem blaming myself. I started battling all kinds of negative thoughts about myself. I would think things like, "maybe I am just not a good preacher," and "maybe I am not good at music and rapping." I felt like I wasn't valuable to anyone and even felt like I was getting too old to be doing what I was doing. I got to the point where I was just beating myself up, and that wasn't getting me anywhere either.

In order to get free from blaming myself, I had to learn to love myself. That was something God had to teach me to do. As I got closer to God, I spent more time alone with Him and became more independent. I started going out by myself, treating myself to dinner, and taking myself out to the movies, and I enjoyed it. I also started making important decisions by myself.

I still had people in my life, but I wasn't depending on them for my happiness or to be responsible for the outcome in my life. I came to a place where I understood that as long as I stayed close to God and continued to listen to His voice and trusted Him to guide me, I would always end up where I was supposed to be. Make a decision today that the "blame game" is over. Forgive people and make a choice not to blame anyone or anything, including yourself for where you are in life. This is very important in living a life of "No Bad Days." You must depend on God above it all. You must know that your relationship with Him and trust in Him is the most important thing.

No matter what you face in your life and no matter who disappoints you, nothing will ever be broken in a way that God can't fix it. Even if you feel the entire world is against you, you have to choose to believe that you and God will always be the majority. Blame over!

CHAPTER 12

Change Your Mind, Change Your Mouth

Your mind records absolutely everything! No matter how long you have been alive, you have spent years seeing and hearing things that are now embedded in your mind. These thoughts can come back at any time and influence how you think and speak without you realizing it. Another way you could have picked up things that you say and believe is by hanging around someone a lot. You may start to sound like them, but don't know it until someone comes up to you and says, "You sound like so and so." Some of you may have had families that passed down their own sayings that have become a part of your belief system that may not be true.

The Bible teaches in-depth about the power of thoughts and words, and I have seen it be true in my life and in the lives of others. If you observe a person who speaks positively, you are likely to find that they experience more positive outcomes. On the other hand, you have probably encountered people in life that are always rehearsing their problems. It seems like they are always going through some kind of drama, and their life matches their words. Some even take ownership of things and make them a part of their identity like sickness and struggle by saying things like, "my depression, my struggles, my pain, etc." Some also have a habit of using absolutes like, "all the time" and "never."

Earlier in the book, I shared about how my tax returns always got used up because problems would show up every year. After I changed what I believed and spoke over the situation, the situation changed! That was not coincidental. I changed my thoughts and my words, and I put a stop to the cycle. You can do this by learning to question and filter your thoughts and words before you respond to them or put them into action.

Step one is understanding that those thoughts are there and will pop up from time to time. Let me give you a great example of how your thoughts from years ago can show up when you least expect them to and shift your whole focus. I remember being in church one day and listening to the pastor preach. All of a sudden, scenes from a horror film I watched twenty years ago begin to play out in my mind with all kinds of profanity. One of the lines in the movie even said something derogatory about Jesus! The same scene played out several times in my mind while the pastor was preaching. It was difficult to make it stop but, eventually, it did, and God spoke to me at that moment and said, "what you put in your mind can show up at any time."

There is a scripture that tells us that we have to capture our thoughts and make them obedient to Christ. (2 Corinthians 10:5) The Bible also talks about having a "carnal mind" vs a "spiritual mind." A carnal mind is moved by the human nature. The spiritual mind is moved by the spiritual nature, which is awakened through a relationship with God and powered by learning His Word. The Bible goes on to say that the carnal mind leads to death, but the spiritual mind leads to life and peace. (Romans 8:6-10) This lets us know that everything we think needs to be tested to figure out whether it came from the carnal mind or from the spiritual mind.

Your mind has both a carnal and spiritual appetite. One of the ways you feed the carnal mind is by looking at and listening to things that appeal to your selfish nature. The kinds of things that will make you want to go get what you want at any cost, as long as you can be satisfied. Another way you feed the carnal mind is to give your attention to negative things that have the power to stir up strife and anger in you. Those kinds of things may make you feel like it is ok to treat people bad, stir up arguments, or even start a fight.

Finally, one of the worst ways you can empower your carnal mind is to fill it up on things that feed fear! Whether it is watching horror films, negative news reports of crime and disasters, or maybe just rehearsing all the trauma you have already been through in life you are feeding the carnal mind. The more you do these things, the stronger fear will become in your life.

On the other hand, there are many ways you can feed your spiritual mind. The Bible says that faith comes by hearing and hearing the Word of God. (Romans 10:17) The spiritual mind is ultimately powered by faith. So, the most important thing is to learn God's Word. Rehearse what you read and replace those negative things with the Word of God. When you feed your spiritual mind, the more you will become prone to doing things God's way.

Where you may have been more self-centered and careless about how your actions affect others, you will become more concerned and compassionate. Where you may have wanted to be mad at someone before, you will find yourself more willing to love and forgive them. Where you used to respond to difficult situations with fear and anxiety, you will find yourself responding with faith.

You can tell which nature you are feeding the most by what words are coming out of your mouth. The Bible teaches that your mouth ultimately reveals what's in your thoughts or in other words, your heart. (Proverbs 15:7) As I said earlier, your words also have tremendous power. When you deal with your thoughts, you will also start to deal with your words.

The Bible teaches that words have the power to bring life or death, and what we see in our lives can be a result of those words. (Proverbs 18:21) James 3:5-6 teaches us that our tongue is like a fire that can corrupt our whole body if left untamed. We have to be very careful about how we use our words.

Not only do you have to watch your own thoughts and words, but you also want to be careful about what you receive from other people. When people say something to you, you have to decide whether to receive it or reject it, or I like to say, "knock it down." If someone says something negative to you, knock it down and be aggressive about it. If you don't make a decision to knock it down, it may land in your heart, and in your life. It may start changing your mind and thought process without you realizing it. As an example, a light-hearted conversation may end up with people using derogatory words like "you're dumb, ignorant, clueless, etc."

Words and phrases like these must go somewhere and if not dealt with correctly, may attach to a part of who you are without you even realizing it. You won't know why, but it was that word that was spoken over you that may be causing confusion in some areas of your life. If a person says something to me jokingly like, "Dave, you so stupid." I am knocking it down, "No, I'm not". With a laugh, but I'm serious

I can remember meeting a businessman who was very intelligent and creative, and yet when someone told him he was smart, he said: "That's impossible! My mom says I am stupid." Even despite the fact that I could see how intelligent and creative he was, he couldn't see it himself because of what someone said to him. I have also noticed that no matter how many people say something kind to you, it is easier to believe that one person who says something negative.

This can even be the case if 500 people say you are beautiful, hearing one person say you're ugly could cause you to overlook the 500 and believe the one instead and start changing your life based on what the one person said. If we make sure we knock that word down the second it tries to attach itself to our mind, we can remain unaffected. We must know who we are, based on what God says about us, and be careful not to let anyone "name us." My spiritual father says, "If you don't know who you are, anybody can name you, if anybody can name you, you will answer to anything."

I have learned that one doesn't have to attend every argument that they might be invited to. Proverbs 15:1 says, "A gentle answer deflects anger, but harsh words make tempers flare." (Proverbs 15:1) So when someone approaches us to argue, we don't have to argue back. We can just speak life and watch God bring life to something that could have otherwise meant death. No one can argue with someone that doesn't argue back.

Learning to speak life starts with knowing how important it is, and then effectively making an effort to put it into practice. When we find ourselves saying something, we wish we wouldn't have said, just take a moment and say the opposite until you train yourself to speak life all the time. When you focus on your words, the spirit of God will help you correct the wrong words you speak. He will surround you with people that will help you. It is amazing how the spirit of the Lord will use anything and anyone to help you.

    I want to encourage you to practice thinking and speaking positive and make a commitment to yourself to have put a guard on your thoughts and words. You can also replace some of the things you used to say with something positive that you can say everyday if you have to.

I have made a habit of reciting my own sayings as often as I can. Many times throughout the day I say, "God got me!" And, when I am faced with a challenge, the first thing I know I need to say is, "this is easy for God!" I may make a mistake from time to time, but I am always sure to correct it immediately because I know how important it is and what an impact it can have.

#nobaddays

CONCLUSION

As I said in the introduction, the message in this book has the power to change your life, but reading one time is just the first step. I want to challenge you today to make a decision to embrace the "12 Ways to Have No Bad Days" represented in each chapter of this book as a part of your everyday life! Here is a quick recap:

Understand that **UNEXPECTED** things will happen to everyone at some point. Decide that no matter how hard things get, **QUITTING** is not an option! Learn to master your **RESPONSES** by not letting what happens in a moment, mess up your lifetime. Create a place of **CHANGE** by inviting God in every situation through praise.

Always remember that God has a **PURPOSE** for everything. If you put your trust in Him, it will all work for your good. Know that there is a **PRINCIPLE** in the Bible that can help you overcome every problem you face. No matter how difficult things get, keep

LOVING and leading those who are around you so they don't get unnecessarily damaged by what you're going through.

Always **TRUST** God over everyone. Become **FEARLESS** knowing that when you stay close to God, nothing can touch you outside of His will. **EXPECT** God to show up in every situation you face. Choose not to **BLAME** anyone for where you are in life, knowing God has the final say. Change your **MIND** and your **MOUTH t**o only think and speak the things that are going to bring the outcome you want in life.

Read through these truths over and over again and challenge yourself to apply them. Just like taking medicine to get well, you have to keep up your doses, or when you are working out, you can't just do it one day and be fit. You have to be committed and consistent to get results.

Most importantly, before you do anything else, I want to encourage you to take this moment to invite the ultimate "No Bad Days Coach" to take His place of leadership in this new journey with you. That coach is God and He wants to be there every step of the way as you begin to apply each and everything you learned. Not only will

He guide you, He will strengthen you as you choose to depend on Him to help you live your life with "No Bad Days."

ABOUT THE AUTHOR

David "DPB" Brooks

David Paul Brooks is best known as "DPB" for his many accomplishments in the Gospel Hip

Hop Industry, having worked with well-known secular and Christian artists and made numerous appearances on Billboard charts. DPB is also well known for his ability to not only captivate audiences but also inspire and empower them through his music.

His motivational speaking and teaching have placed him in front of a diversity of audiences, including school assemblies, local churches, and even jails and juvenile detention centers, some of which, as a result of his partnership with local police departments.

DPB is also a Rhema Bible College graduate with a passion for learning and teaching principles that can help people transform their lives and has now extended his reach into writing with the release of his first book, "No Bad Days." For more about DPB log onto www.worldofdpb.com

Made in the USA
Columbia, SC
11 September 2022